SPRING TOOK THE LONG WAY AROUND

ALSO BY BROOKE HERTER JAMES

The Widest Eye (poetry chapbook, 2016)

Why Did the Farmer Cross the Road? (picture book, 2017)

SPRING TOOK THE LONG WAY AROUND

Poems by

Brooke Herter James

Antrim House
Bloomfield, Connecticut

Copyright © 2019 by Brooke Herter James

Except for short selections reprinted for purposes of
book review, all reproduction rights are reserved.
Requests for permission to replicate should
be addressed to the publisher.

ISBN: 978-1-943826-56-8

First Edition, 2019

Printed & bound by Ingram Content Group

Book design by Rennie McQuilkin

Front cover photograph by Sam James

Author photograph by David James

Antrim House
860.217.0023
AntrimHouseBooks@gmail.com
www.AntrimHouseBooks.com
400 Seabury Dr., #5196, Bloomfield, CT 06002

For Dave

I could stand all day
in this glistening river
near you, fisherman

Acknowledgments

Grateful acknowledgment to the editors of the following publications in which these poems first appeared, at times in earlier versions:

Mountain Troubadour Poetry Journal (Poetry Society of Vermont): "Southbound, Maine Turnpike, Labor Day"

Poem Town 2018: "First Snow," "Sun Dog, Wolf Moon"

Poem Town 2019: "Every Morning Now," "Route 90 Westbound," "At the Edge," "Old Bear," "Survival"

Poets Reading the News: "Fires"

With gratitude to my many teachers: my fellow poets of the Woodstock Vermont Poetry Group; my new poet friends from the Key West Literary Seminar; Matthew Lippman of the Gotham Writers' Workshop; Suzy Becker, Sharon Sorokin James and Waleska James of the Mole Hill Writers' Retreat; Rennie McQuilkin of Antrim House; and, finally and always, my beloved David, Sam, Peter, Frances, Ben and Hank.

Table of Contents

It's Quiet Here / 3
Sun Dog, Wolf Moon / 4
First Snow / 5
Bad Poem! / 6
Your First Birthday / 7
At the Edge / 8
Southbound, Maine Turnpike, Labor Day / 9
Route 90 Westbound / 10
Fires / 11
Survival / 12
The Shape of Time / 13
It All Matters / 15
Love in the Time of Cancer / 17
A Wednesday in May / 18
Orchard at Twilight / 20
Epiphany / 21
Untitled / 22
Old Bear / 24
Spring took the long way around / 26
Every Morning Now / 27

About the Author / 29
About the Book / 30

Speak ye well of the meadow mice,
wee things to have weathered the freeze
with breath enough to spare
to leave a rime like stars
above each burrow in the field.
Bring gifts, bow down, and learn.

                              Rennie McQuilkin

SPRING TOOK THE LONG WAY AROUND

It's Quiet Here

I am going to sit all day
on this hay bale. No better place
to be. Here in the barn,
spiders drop down from dusty
rafters on invisible threads,
chickens scratch at rotten cucumbers
from last summer's garden,
the donkeys stand side by side,
their faces to the warmth
of an early October sun. It's quiet here.
Maybe in an hour I will wander
back to the kitchen and refill
my cup with coffee.

Sun Dog, Wolf Moon

We woke to a Sun Dog
splitting the sky,
three suns out of one,
a halo of light enshrouding
the sugar maple at the edge
of the snowy drive.
Must be the cold, we said
as we stood in awe.
I had seen cold work its magic before.
Diamond dust in the Gallatin Valley.
But this was something else,
this being the last day
of the year and all.
Later we returned from evening chores,
the donkeys fed and watered,
our breaths shortened by the crystalline freeze.
Behind us a Wolf Moon rose
silent and huge over the barn to the east,
throwing our shadows down long before us
as if to say *stay awake.*

First Snow

First snow falling
fast and furious
this early December
morning in Vermont.
The donkeys huddled
inside the barn,
the dog running circles
in joyous disbelief
at the transformation
of his world.
Me, too.
Much needed:
this new landscape
I woke to,
November's detritus
buried and forgiven.
This is not the poem
I would have written yesterday
when fallen apples lay abandoned;
nor the poem I will write tomorrow
when the smooth white is plowed and piled.
This is the poem for now,
in gratitude for the miracle
of this first snow.

Bad Poem!

The words just slide
off the page, one
after another, tiny
black lemmings racing
for the edge of the desk,
ignoring my pleas for just
one more try. They are gone,
whole stanzas deconstructing mid-air,
couplets de-coupling,
rhymes un-rhyming,
metaphors set free,
quick brown foxes
jumping over the lazy
dog at my feet, the dog
who never opens an eye
even as a clumsy gerund
catches in his whiskers
on its way to the floor.
I crawl on hands and knees
collecting what I can.
I leave it all in a heap
on the blotter and go out
for a walk.
The dog comes, too.

Your First Birthday

The miniature Happy Birthday
banner hangs from orange wooden
toothpicks planted in gooey
frosted cake, the candle leaning,
your tiny pointer finger close
to the flame while we in our
silly hats and ribbon necklaces
circle in close and sing to you,
to us, to mothers and fathers,
grandparents and aunts,
to uncles, to friends with babies,
friends without, to sweet dogs,
cozy pajamas, hot chocolate,
the surprise in your eyes.

Years later I look at the photograph.
It is just as I remember
except this: We are not there.
It is only you and your mother
and the gift of a cake.

At the Edge

So certain he is by day,
his job to flush chickadees
from the crabapple tree,
chase leaves as they
float off the maple,
dig holes under the porch.
When his work is done,
the food bowl is full,
the water clean and cold,
the praise abundant and tender
as he sits and stays.
If only when deep darkness comes
they would shut the windows,
draw the curtains,
read aloud to one another
as he lies at the foot of their bed
trying not to hear
the yip, the howl, the bay
at the pitch-
dark edge of his wildness.

Southbound, Maine Turnpike, Labor Day

Give me big black crows on the Route 95 median strip and
I will give you twelve years old lining the cracked back seat
armrest of our station wagon with the peppermints
I've licked out of my HoJo's ice cream cone staring out
the open window on the long hot tar drive home from summer
listening to my parents natter thinking about what I will wear
to the first day of school if there's any mail waiting for me
if my room will smell like late August grape jelly if my fish tank
will be slime green if a boy with a lisp will stand under the street light
tonight and call out my name.

Give me big black crows on the Route 95 median strip and
I will give you sixteen and three quarters still sucking on peppermint
bits thinking about the first day of school where my locker will be
who's in my homeroom begging my mother to turn the radio dial
my father to drive faster so I can take the car to the mall navigating 287
or the Saw Mill windows down diet coke between my legs the boy
with the lisp replaced by the boy whose musty wool scarf
I keep under my pillow.

Give me big black crows on the Route 95 median strip one year later and
I will give you my father living somewhere else my sister too now
my mother driving so slowly hands at eleven and one cigarette burning
wanting to play the license plate game
me sitting in the front seat bare feet on the dashboard hating the taste
of the words in my head wishing for something I can't name.

Route 90 Westbound

Route 90 westbound,
rolling up miles of blacktop river
through chickpea farms, feed lots,
slaughterhouses, the Mississippi behind,
the Yellowstone ahead. In between,
the promise of Wall Drug, cheap gas,
Upick strawberries, tattoo removals, corn
dogs, porn shops and life without crystal meth.
Jesus everywhere, crackling
on the AM/FM/XM dials, peeling off billboards,
smiling up from truck stop placemats,
coffee stain halos and all.
Checking out of the Comfort Inn
to the pink of early sky,
I smell rain somewhere to the west.

Fires

Those were the fire years.
Fires first in the mountains.
Lightning strikes in the distance
glowing, red orange sunrises and sunsets.
Fires down in the valleys,
whole mountains disappearing
behind smoky clouds.
Fires we thought we understood.
But then came the flames in little towns
on blue sky days. Spontaneous ignition
on leafy suburban streets,
on city sidewalks, on park benches,
on football fields. Fires around dinner
tables, in diners, on buses,
in classrooms and courtrooms and churches.
Fires everywhere burning everything
we knew and loved to ash. Later, we dug
through the remains looking for clues.
We found anger,
buried alive.

Survival

Once she had cancer.
It tried to eat her cell by
cell from the inside out.
She rode the conveyor belt
of malignancy eradication,
nudged along by white coats
and silver machines,
stumbling off at the end of a year,
blinking into the sunshine,
snipping off her plastic id band,
hopping into the waiting car,
speeding down the highway,
windows open.
Lunch at Five Guys: juicy burgers,
salty fries. And then
Lake Street Dive came on the radio,
the very same song she heard every day
lying alone in a room so lit up
everyone else had to leave.
She heard the first chords and had
to pull over while she retched her insides
out into the purple chicory.

I wonder if this is what survival feels like -
the sour taste in the mouth,
the shudder, the revulsion
at the piece of us that's already
surrendered to the death
that hasn't yet happened.

The Shape of Time

Ask me the shape of time and
I will draw you a perfect circle,
a year pinned in place,
the left side colonized
by autumn months,
the right by spring,
the crown leisurely
reserved for summer,
the base a slushy mess.

If I fold my year in half,
October touches April
and vernal buds blush
at the brush of fall's
red leaves. Flocks of geese
fill both skies, restless warblers
hop from spring twig to autumn
branch and back again.
If I fold my year
top to bottom instead,
long, verdant days stretch
their sleeveless arms around
hurried weeks of head-down,
collar-up cold.

By some synesthetic
sleight of hand, summer lasts
the longest and I can ride

my red Raleigh bicycle
across the arc of my year,
squeezing the hand brakes,
dragging my sneakers on the sun-
baked blacktop, slowing
down the fall.

It All Matters

The next time someone says
There's no There, There,
as in *Whatever* or *Who Cares?*
I will respond by saying
(politely) *au contraire.*
And then I will point
to the period at the end
of this sentence.
See that? I will say.
That, right THERE, is the
size of a moss piglet,
a moss piglet that might
very well be on this page
right now, or in the rain drop
on your window screen
or swimming at the bottom
of your coffee cup
or napping in lichen
on the north side of
that log you meant to cut
for firewood last summer.
Right now, right here is a jolly
and fat and puffed all day long
like a marshmallow-man
moss piglet that loves to cuddle
with its partner in the Himalayas

or swim 4000 meters under the sea,
and, oh, did I mention it has survived
all five great extinctions, and will be
most certainly riding a teardrop
down our collective cheeks
if we don't stop the sixth?
Okay, now you've got me
on a rant, when what I really
want to say is: *It's all Here, Here*
and it all matters.
Period.

Love in the Time of Cancer

After nearly forty years
whatever space remains
between them, gone.
His body wraps
around her so,
his ten fingers
lie atop each of hers.

Sweet air slips in.
When she wakes again,
curtains open,
coffee on the bedside table,
she hears the screen door open.
A dog barks.

Then summer happens after all,
picking raspberries,
swimming in the pond,
and before they know it,
it's Standard Time once again
and Thanksgiving's on its way.

A Wednesday in May

A lilac-infused Wednesday in May,
grocery list on the seat beside me,
a one-finger wave to the road crew
on route 100 as I drive by.
Then there he is,
lying perfectly in the middle
of my lane, so perfectly
I don't even have to swerve.

In the produce aisle,
searching for leafy greens,
I recall his face pointed skywards,
tiny paws touching one another
across his soft grey breast
as if sunbathing on the warm
black pavement, or nodding off,
three pages into a new book.

Like my father, eyes paler blue
than his faded striped cotton pajamas,
his long fingers intertwined
across his quiet chest, nails trim and
clean. Music drifts from the kitchen radio,
mingles with the smell of city -
pavement and garbage trucks and coffee.
I lean in to smooth the sheets.

One hour later on my way home,
windows open, hot tar

shimmering and workmen
sitting on tailgates,
the squirrel is still there.
Dozens of cars must have straddled
his tiny body, dozens of drivers like me
wishing not to disturb his death.

Orchard at Twilight

At dusk we sat in the courtyard,
rubbed our stockinged feet,
weary of cobblestone streets.
We drank wine from
thick-rimmed goblets,
shut our eyes, dreamt.
Where are the children?
You with a lantern
offered to collect them
from the orchard down the lane
where they played with the goats
and hung from the trees.
Then there they were -
barefoot, laughing, faces
and fingers plum purple,
juices dripping from their chins.

Epiphany

I was eight when Liz Mahoney's father died.
I sat on a hard bench pew in the
Presbyterian Church on Broadway
and cried so hard my mother placed
a grey-gloved hand on my back
to still my shuddering spine.
Later, as she tucked me into bed,
she explained that sometimes
when you start crying about one thing
you end up crying about every sadness
you have ever known - which gave me pause,
as until that day all I had known of misery
was the demise of my dime store turtle.
Sad as that was, his life under the palm tree
must have been okay and the funeral procession
to his grave under the rhododendron
was magnificent. I lay still in the darkness as
my mother crossed the room, turning to say she loved me.
That's when I knew she was wrong.
The sadness is about what's yet to come.

Untitled

I see you
touch your tiny finger
to the green rubber tip
of your sneaker as you say
> *shoe*
> *shoe*
> *shoe*

and I think of my father
in the last year of his life
tapping the clean trimmed nail
of his right pointer finger
against the car window,
reading out loud every sign
as we pass by.
> *Route 495*
> *Hebert's Candies*
> *Wissel's Junk Shop*

Then at dinner
he's quiet,
having lost the word
for the dish of vegetables
he wishes to try.
If only you had been there
to prompt him,
across the table
in your highchair

dropping
> *Peas*
> *Peas*
> *Peas*

onto the wooden floor.

> *Ah yes! Peas!*

He would have laughed, too -
you and he
unlikely confederates
in the ordination of this world.

Old Bear

When I was young
I welcomed the gift,

the long rest after
months of foraging,

tearing bark from trees
in early spring, digging

sweet roots of Jack-
in-the-pulpit, feasting

off blueberries, beech nuts,
acorns from leafy groves.

I ate until sated, then slept,
curled on a mossy bed

beneath the upturned roots
of a white pine felled

by September winds.
I slept hard and long

until the scent of evaporating snow
filled my nostrils and the earth

dampened beneath me. I woke
to a slant of light, having dreamt

of skunk cabbage, hungry once more.
Now I am old. I dread the first snow

piling high in these quieting woods,
only the chickadees to scold me

as I trudge along
in search of tender twigs.

I don't want to prepare my bed
for a long winter's nap in this hollow,

deep in the woods. Not yet.
I would like to sit awhile,

back against a limbless snag.
I would like to stay awake

to hear clumps of snow slide
from the spruce's silvery arms,

to watch moonlight catch beech leaves
shivering in the cold.

Spring took the long way around

this year, a shy schoolgirl
lingering along field's edge
as the boisterous ones
gather their sleds, hang skates
off hockey sticks, suck snow
from soggy wool mittens and wander off.
They stayed too long and they know it,
but the ice was so black and smooth.
They call over their shoulders at the girl
hesitating by the stone wall,
We're done here, it's all yours.
She waits to be sure
they are gone for good.
Then, holding her skirts high
above soft snow, she ambles across the pasture.
This is mine now she thinks as she breathes
her warm breath such that the maples
blush red at their tips and the last ice
melts from the pond.

Every Morning Now

the donkey wanders
from the barn
to the apple tree
on the path
they made together.
She stops
just shy of the fence,
leaving room for her
misplaced donkey friend.

I imagine you
or I
will do the same,
will forever
pour coffee for two.

ABOUT THE AUTHOR

Brooke Herter James won her first creative writing award in eighth grade and her second many decades later. In between, she followed a circuitous path that included college, graduate school, public health nursing, and raising a family. Eight years ago, she remembered that grade school story and decided to circle back to what she loves to do most. *Spring Took the Long Way Around* is her second collection of poems. She is also the author of the children's picture book *Why Did the Farmer Cross the Road?* She is an active member of the Society of Children's Book Writers and Illustrators, a student in the Gotham Writers' Workshop, a graduate of the Yale Writers' Conference, and an enthusiastic member of the Woodstock Poetry Group. She lives in a very old house in Vermont with her husband, two donkeys, four chickens and a dog named Mack. (Actually, the donkeys and chickens live in the barn.)

This book is set in Garamond Premier Pro, which had its genesis in 1988 when type-designer Robert Slimbach visited the Plantin-Moretus Museum in Antwerp, Belgium, to study its collection of Claude Garamond's metal punches and typefaces. During the mid-fifteen hundreds, Garamond—a Parisian punch-cutter—produced a refined array of book types that combined an unprecedented degree of balance and elegance, for centuries standing as the pinnacle of beauty and practicality in type-founding. Slimbach has created an entirely new interpretation based on Garamond's designs and on compatible italics cut by Robert Granjon, Garamond's contemporary.

This book is available at all bookstores.

•

On the house website
(www.antrimhousebooks.com)
in addition to information on books
you will find sample poems, upcoming events,
and a "seminar room" featuring supplemental biography,
notes, images, poems, reviews, and
writing suggestions.

www.ingramcontent.com/pod-product-compliance
Lightning Source LLC
Chambersburg PA
CBHW030104100526
44591CB00008B/272